The
CAGED
System
for Guitar

A clear-cut guide
to learning the entire
guitar fretboard

BY PETE MADSEN

ISBN 978-1-4234-6173-9

HAL•LEONARD®
7777 W. BLUEMOUND RD. P.O. BOX 13819 MILWAUKEE, WI 53213

In Australia Contact:
Hal Leonard Australia Pty. Ltd.
4 Lentara Court
Cheltenham, Victoria, 3192 Australia
Email: ausadmin@halleonard.com.au

Visit Hal Leonard Online at
www.halleonard.com

TABLE OF CONTENTS

	Page	Track

INTRODUCTION

Those of you familiar with the first position chords C, A, G, E, and D may not know it, but you have a powerful tool at your disposal for navigating the entire fretboard. These simple chord shapes can be repeated all over the neck, allowing you to play several different "voicings" of the same chord and create chord inversions (same chord but with the notes arranged in a different order). Why is this valuable? Well, let's say we are playing a simple three-chord song with C, F, and G chords. You're playing the third verse, and say to yourself, "I need to make this more interesting…increase the drama." If you can move the same three chords up the neck, the sound automatically becomes more interesting because the higher pitched notes give the impression of "movement" within the piece without overcomplicating things.

There are several books and internet sites that describe the CAGED system in significant detail. However, few (if any) give the student concrete examples of how to apply the system. In this book, we will examine the basic system as it applies to major chords, minor chords, and seventh chords, then apply that knowledge with chord progressions, songs, and riffs. Whether you realize it or not, every scale, riff, or lick that you play or hear can be related to one or more of these five CAGED chord shapes. It is my hope that, after reading through and playing the examples in this book, you will gain the knowledge to take this system and apply it to any playing situation—whether that be as a composer, improviser, or just somebody who wants a better appreciation of how the guitar fretboard is laid out.

I play a fair amount of fingerpicking blues and have found the CAGED system invaluable as a resource for coming up with interesting variations on the standard three-chord, 12-bar blues form. Indeed, I feel the true strength of the CAGED system lies in exploring the possibilities of simpler song structures, such as those found in blues, rock, and popular music; I also believe that it can provide insight for the guitarist in any playing situation, whether that be in blues, rock, jazz, or classical styles.

Part of the beauty of CAGED is that, at its core, it reduces the guitar down to five simple visual components: a C chord, an A chord, a G chord, an E chord, and a D chord. From there, we can expand outward to grasp as much of the complexity of the instrument as we wish. Most people are visually inclined and can lock into this system of chord shapes easier than, say, having a teacher explain a lot of theory, which assumes a level of abstraction that may or may not be useful to the student.

Of course, having some theoretical knowledge is useful, so at the end of the book, you will find an appendix devoted to explaining how chords are built. It's placed at the end so that you can use it as a reference or tackle it at a time when it suits you. Keep in mind: the CAGED system is a VISUAL system, but music is heard and not seen. The chord shapes are consistent in their relationship to each other, but the notes—the actual pitches we hear—will be different depending on where the shapes are played on the neck. This concept is crucial to developing a thorough command of the fretboard.

HOW TO USE THIS BOOK

It is most useful to work through the first three chapters of the book to try and understand how the CAGED system works as applied to major, minor, and seventh chords. You might want to start with the C chord shapes for each chapter, as I have done, and then work through the remaining A, G, E, and D chord shapes. You can, of course, work in the sharp and flat keys as you find time to do so. It is important to spend time playing in all keys—not just the ones that are most familiar—in order to become a more well-rounded musician.

Once you feel that you have a firm grasp of how the system works, move on to the playing examples in Chapters 4, 5, and 6. These examples apply the concepts you've learned in more realistic musical examples.

ACKNOWLEDGMENTS

I would like to thank my guitar students for letting me bounce CAGED ideas off them, Chad Johnson for the useful edits, and Catherine and Nicolas, my inspiration.

CHAPTER 1:
The CAGED System and Major Chords

The CAGED Skeleton

Example 1 lays out the bare bones skeleton of the system. You probably already know these chords: C–A–G–E–D. What you may not know is that you can work these chord **shapes** in this order up the neck to get higher or lower pitched voicings of the same chords. Notice I said shapes instead of actual chords. This is the most important concept of this lesson: we need to shift our thinking from "this is a C chord" to "this is a C chord **shape**," because we will be moving the different shapes up the neck to produce entirely different chords from what you might be used to.

But first thing's first. Here are the five open-position chords for review: C, A, G, E, and D.

EXAMPLE **1**

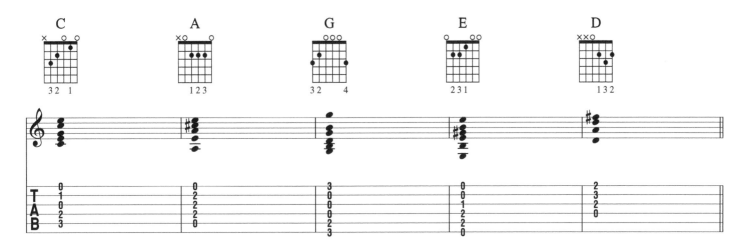

What's important to realize when making use of these shapes elsewhere on the neck, is that the open strings should be thought of as a fret. To see what I mean, play these five chords again, but re-finger them without using your first finger, instead laying it behind the nut, as if barring. That's how these shapes become moveable.

EXAMPLE **1A**

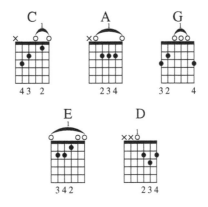

Five Different C Chords

In **Example 2**, we see two versions, or "voicings," of a C chord. The first shape is the one most guitarists are used to. Now take a look at the second shape. Compare the sound of this chord against the open C chord. These two chords produce a similar sound—they're both made of the same notes! You can think of this second chord as a C chord using an "A shape." Compare this chord shape to the A chord in **Example 1A**, and you should see the familiar form; we've just slid it up a few frets to make it a C chord.

EXAMPLE 2

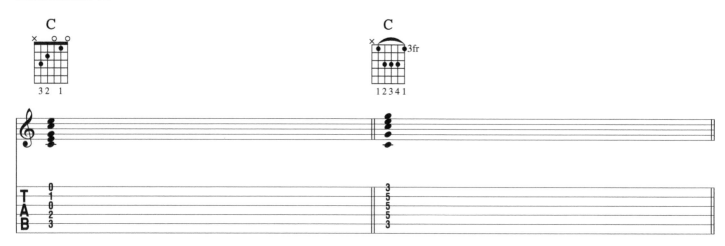

Here are two very common variations on this A-form shape. The first leaves off the top string, allowing you to barre strings 4, 3, and 2 with your third finger, while the second leaves off the fifth string, which eliminates the need for a barre.

EXAMPLE 2A

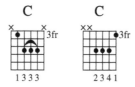

Before we go any further, we should look at which notes make up a C chord. There are three notes: C, E, and G. Even though we may be playing four, five, or six strings, we are actually only playing these three notes; it's just that some of them are repeated in different octaves. For example, in our first position C chord, starting from the fifth string, we are playing in order: C (5), E (4), G (3), C (2), and E (1). Notice we play the C and E notes twice.

In the A-shape C chord, we are playing, from the fifth string: C (5), G (4), C (3), E (2), and G (1). These are the same three notes, but just in a different order. In our open C chord, we double the notes C and E in different octaves. In the A-shape C chord, we double the notes C and G in different octaves; this gives you a slightly different sound.

In **Example 3**, we'll play a C chord using a G shape. Notice I have written out three versions of this chord. The reason is that the first version is very difficult to play and therefore, not very practical. In fact, I expect that many players simply won't be able to perform the large finger stretch this requires. However, it's listed here for you to see that it actually is a G shape. Again, compare to the G chord in **Example 1A** to see the basic form.

The next two versions of this chord strip away, one string at a time, the lower notes, so the third version is one you might find the most practical. It's still a bit of a stretch, but it's certainly easier than the first one.

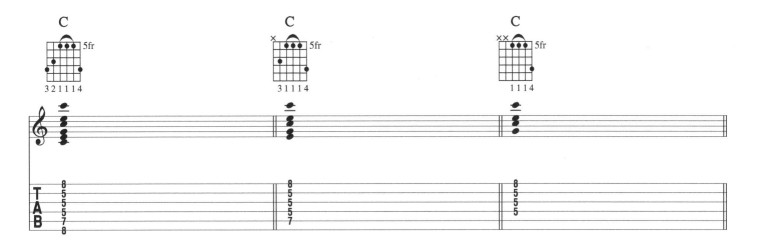

If you look closely, you can see how this resembles the A shape we played in **Example 2**; the notes on strings 4, 3, and 2 are all played at the same fret.

It's All Connected

This brings me to another important point: we can use each shape within the CAGED system to connect to the next shape. This is important because when we start to form new chords, we can find the next shape via the "connected" note, thus learning to navigate the fretboard! As we just saw, the G shape is connected to the A shape via strings 4, 3, and 2, but how does the open C shape connect to the A shape? The lowest note of both chord forms is the same C note on the fifth string (circled in diagrams). Check out **Example 4** to see this.

EXAMPLE 4

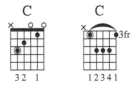

Another connection is common as well. In **Example 4A**, I am giving you a slightly different version of the open C shape. If you add your pinky to the first string at the fret 3, you have added another G note. (Remember, C, E, and G make up a C chord.) This G note (circled in diagrams) will also connect you to the A-shape of C.

Example 4A

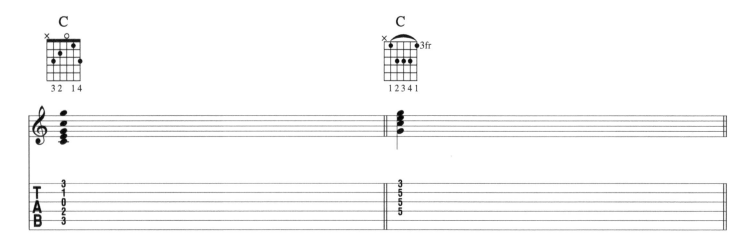

Let's move on to the final E and D shapes. In **Example 5**, you can easily recognize the first shape, the E shape, as a standard barre chord. This requires a good bit of hand strength, and if barre chords are new to you, I suggest working with this about five to ten minutes a day over several weeks. The slight, temporary discomfort is well worth it, as these barre chord shapes are extremely valuable.

Be sure to notice that the E shape is connected to our previous G shape at the C note on the first string, eighth fret. Moving forward, we can see that the E shape is connected to the D shape via the tenth-fret C note on string 4 (circled in diagrams).

Example 5

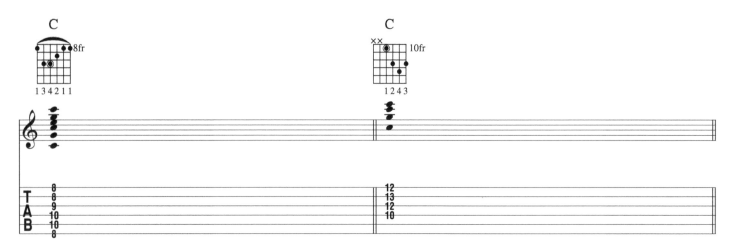

Strumming Examples

Now let's try some strumming exercises to see how these chord shapes might sound in a song. In **Example 6**, we'll strum each chord in quarter notes. We start out with the open-position C chord, move to an A-shape C chord, then to the G shape, and finally to the E shape. If you notice, I've abbreviated the E-shape C chord by eliminating the two lowest strings (strings 6 and 5). In fact, this shape might look familiar to those of you who know a first-position F chord.

EXAMPLE 6
TRACK 2

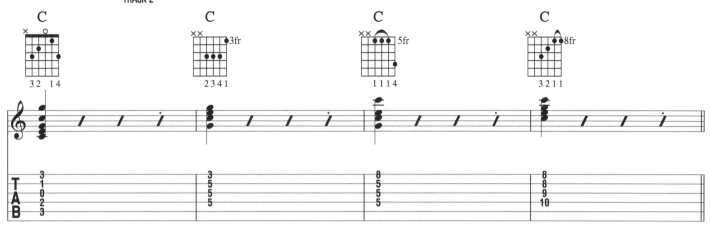

We've been bangin' away on C for a while now, so let's try this with an F chord. In **Example 7**, the common first-position F chord is actually based off an E shape; we've just eliminated the two lowest strings. The next shape would be a D shape. Since the full D shape, with the index finger fretting the F note on string 4, fret 3, is a little difficult, I've given you the option of using the D shape F chord by using the top three strings only—it's still an F chord.

In the CAGED model with the C chord, we didn't talk about moving from the D shape back to the C shape because we ran out of room on the fretboard (or at least on most acoustic fretboards). The system does repeat itself, and we can see that here with the F chord in measure 3. When moving from the D shape to the C shape, you can see that they're connected via the top three strings.

This C-shape F chord requires a barre across the top three strings with your index finger while handling the notes on strings 2, 4, and 5 with fingers 2, 3, and 4, respectively. Again, this is a bit of a difficult shape, so you can eliminate the pinky on string 5, and have a much easier chord to use.

EXAMPLE 7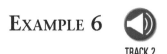

TRACK 3

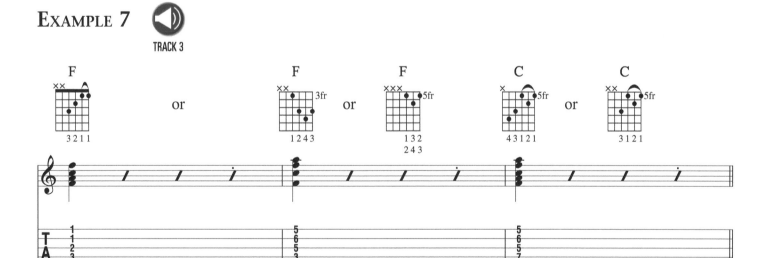

Example 8 is a simple eight-measure progression on which to practice your new CAGED skills. The strumming pattern throughout is: down, down-up, down, down. We'll be changing chord shapes every two beats so that we get a sense of melodic movement within this piece. Even though we're using just three chords (C, F, and G), it sounds like more is going on because of the different shapes.

Try playing through this at a nice, slow tempo. Then, using the same chord progression, try substituting different chord shapes. For instance, in the first four measures of the song, we play one measure of C using two shapes (A shape and C shape) and one measure of F using two shapes (E shape and D shape). Now try using G and E shapes for the C chord in measure 1, and A and C shapes for the F chord in measure 2.

EXAMPLE 8

TRACK 4

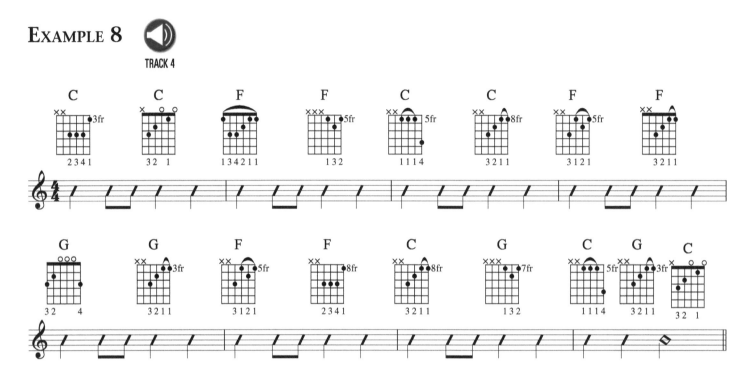

You can expand this workout quite a bit by picking some of your favorite songs and applying the CAGED method to the chord changes. Who knows—it might just perk up your ears for some incredible new musical possibilities.

In **Example 9**, we see an A chord put through the CAGED forms. Starting with the A shape, we move through G, E, D, and C forms.

EXAMPLE 9

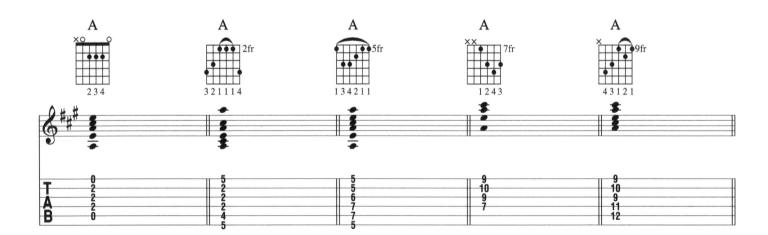

And here's the CAGED system applied to G chords.

Example 10

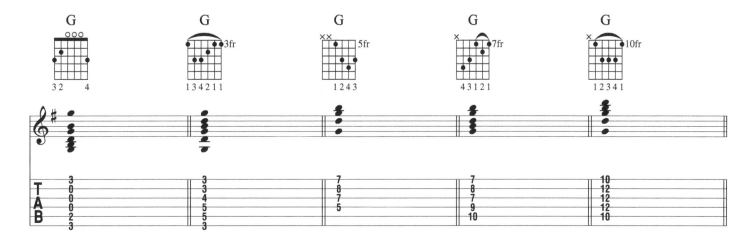

CHAPTER 2:
CAGED Minor Chords

Now let's turn our attention to minor chords, which have a darker, sadder sound than major chords. This is due to the root-minor 3rd relationship, as opposed to the root-major 3rd relationship of major chords. Don't worry too much about what this means now; just be sure to note the difference in sound between the two. You can use any adjectives you'd like to describe the difference: major = happy, uplifting, bright; minor = sad, brooding, dark, etc.

As with major chords, most of these shapes will be familiar, although a few of them may be new. Most people know Am, Em, and Dm open chords, and will therefore recognize them as moveable chord forms. The Cm and Gm open chords are much less common though, and there's good reason for that. They aren't exactly finger-friendly or very well suited for strumming around the campfire. However, they can be effective shapes to use for arpeggio riffs.

EXAMPLE 1

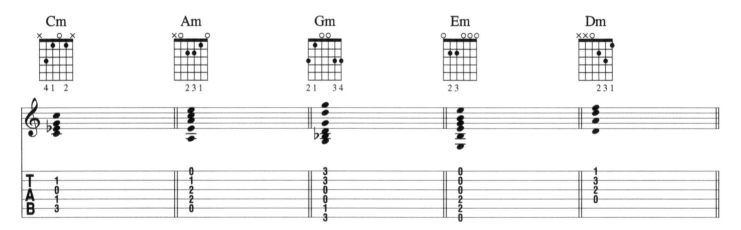

Five Different Cm Chords

So now let's create five different C minor chords using these shapes. In **Example 2**, be sure to notice the notes that connect the shapes throughout.

EXAMPLE 2

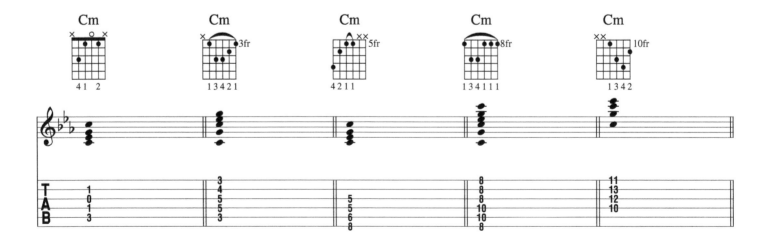

Example 3 shows the CAGED shapes applied to an Am chord. We start with the A shape and progress through G, E, D, and C shapes.

EXAMPLE 3

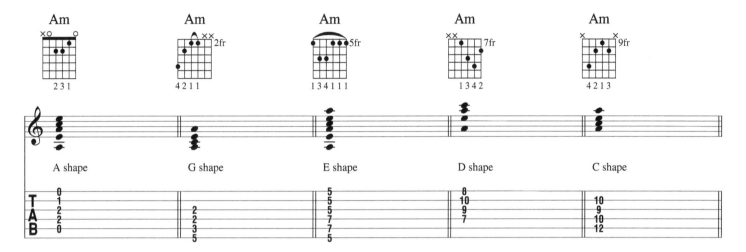

Strumming Exercise

Now let's try a simple strumming exercise using all minor chords. **Example 4** uses several different forms for Dm and Am chords. Can you figure out which forms they are? (Answers appear below example.)

EXAMPLE 4
TRACK 5

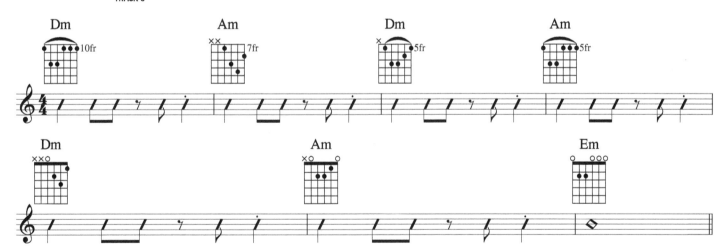

Measure 1 = E-shape Dm, 2 = D-shape Am, 3 = A-shape Am, 4 = E-shape Dm, 5 = D-shape Dm, 6 = A-shape Am, 7 = E-shape Em.

Arpeggio Exercise

Example 5 takes the G-shape minor chord form and moves it up and down the neck for different minor chord arpeggios.

EXAMPLE 5

TRACK 6

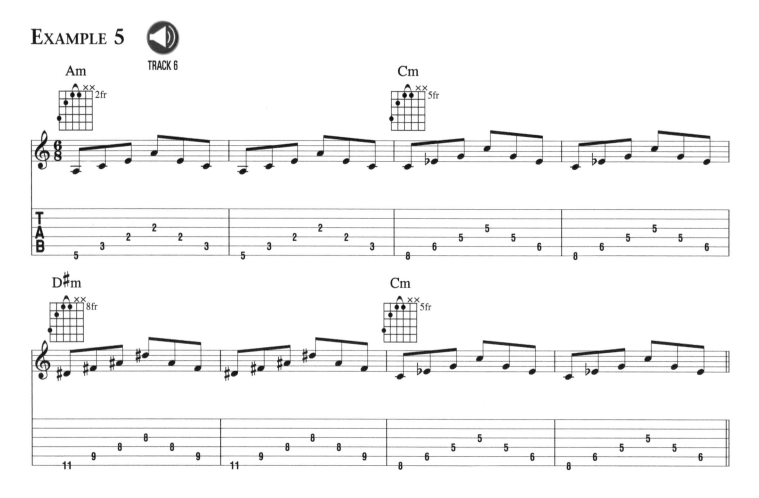

CHAPTER 3:
CAGED Seventh Chords

Aside from major or minor chords, seventh chords are the most useful chords to know. They're based off major or minor chords but have one additional note. Major and minor chords are more specifically called *triads* because they contain three different notes: a root, a 3rd, and a 5th. A major triad contains a major 3rd, while a minor triad contains a minor 3rd. To create a seventh chord (specifically a dominant seventh chord), we add a ♭7th note on top of a major triad.

Again, don't worry too much about completely understanding the theory behind this yet—just try to become familiar with the sound of seventh chords. To my ear, they sound like a major chord that's slightly unresolved, thus providing an intriguing tension. Here are the open-position seventh chords in our CAGED sequence.

EXAMPLE 1

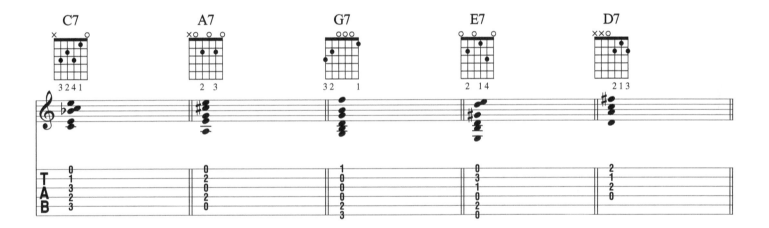

Five Different C7 Chords

In **Example 2**, we see the CAGED sequence applied to C chords to create five different C7 chords. The G shape is a bit difficult, so I'll show you a way to abbreviate that one later.

EXAMPLE 2

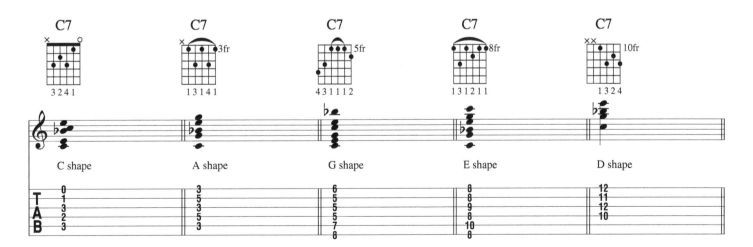

Example 3 demonstrates the CAGED sequence applied to A7 chords.

EXAMPLE 3

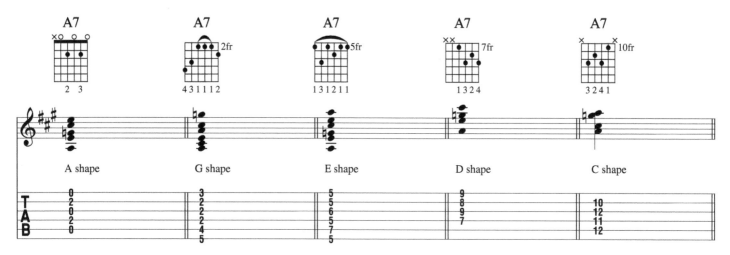

A shape   G shape   E shape   D shape   C shape

Strumming Exercise

Example 4 is a short strumming example to give you a small taste of how seventh chords sound in context.

EXAMPLE 4

TRACK 7

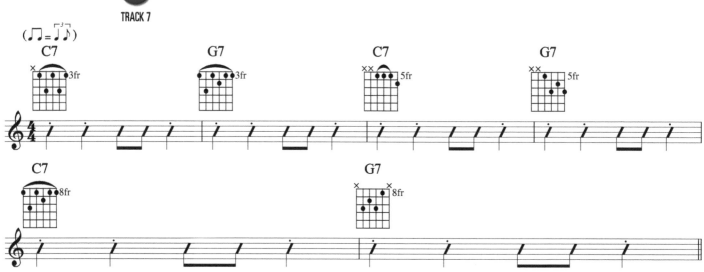

CHAPTER 4:
Song Structures

Knowing the CAGED system is great. You may have already worked out a lot of the connections, but without practical playing experience, it can seem like just another bunch of esoteric information. In this chapter, we're going to take some common chord changes found in hundreds (maybe thousands) of songs and apply CAGED shapes. In this way, while the actual chord structure does not change, the song continues to evolve because the chord voicings change.

SONG 1

TRACK 8

Our first song takes the chord progression G–Em–C–Am and uses a simple strumming pattern. After four measures, we repeat the progression but change the shapes. We start out with normal open chords. Then, we change to an E-shape G, a D-shape Em, an A-shape C, and an E-shape Am. In the last four measures, we use a D-shape G, an A-shape Em, an E-shape C, and a D-shape Am.

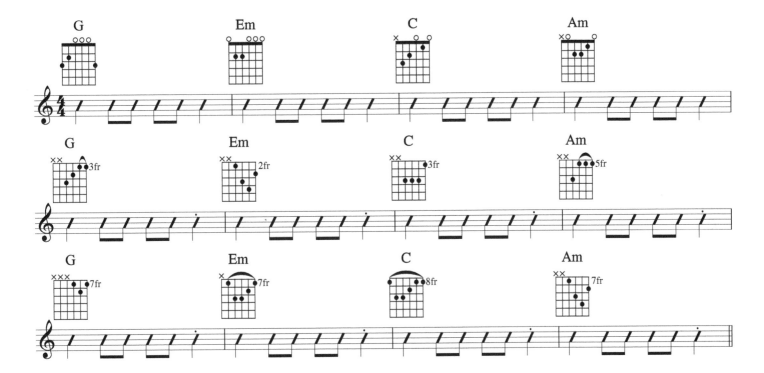

SONG 2

Song 2 uses an A–C#m–F#m–E progression. We start out with an open A chord, then move into an A-shape C#m chord. This is followed with an E-shape F#m chord and an open E chord. In the four measures, the A chord moves to an E-shape, and the C#m stays put. Then, we move that C#m up to the ninth fret for F#m. Finally, the E chord uses an A shape at the seventh fret. In the final four measures, we use smaller chords all centered around the ninth fret. The D-shape A chord is first, followed by the E-shape C#m, the same F#m chord from the previous group but pared down to just three strings, and a G-shape E chord with the two low strings eliminated.

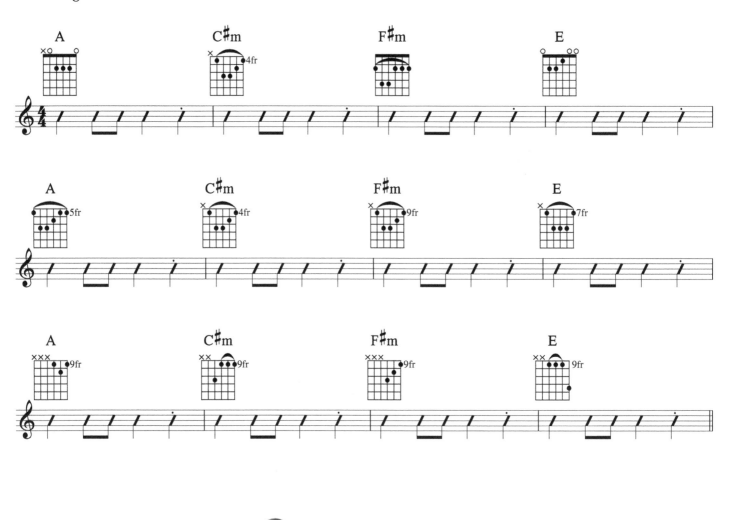

SONG 3

Many songs consist of nothing but I, IV, and V chords; the progression is common throughout blues, rock, and pop music. **Song 3** demonstrates how a pedestrian G–C–D progression (I–IV–V) can be made to sound a bit more fresh by employing some CAGED chord shapes.

By this point, you should be getting pretty good at recognizing the forms, so I'll stop naming them, but that doesn't mean you should stop. Be sure to recognize each chord form and make mental notes to yourself along the way until it becomes second nature.

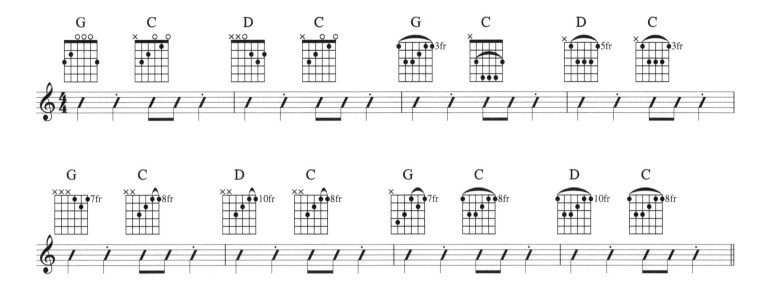

SONG 4

TRACK 11

In **Song 4**, we have another I–IV–V progression, this time in E. We'll use a continuous down-up strumming pattern in eighth notes and two variations on the open chord shapes with which we begin. The A-shape B and E chords used have a nice rock feel and punchy sound. For the A and B chords at the end, which use the D shape, the notes on the top strings are optional. It will sound a little rock 'n' roll to leave them off.

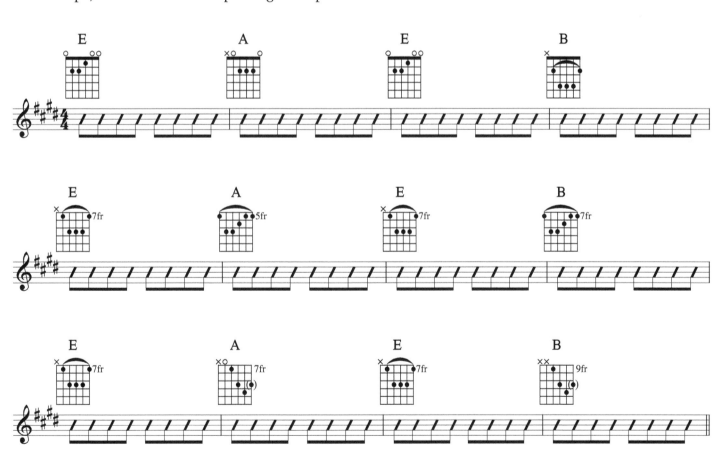

SONG 5

In **Song 5**, we'll be playing some arpeggios. For each chord, we'll use the same picking pattern: down-down-down, up-up-up. This example is in 6/8 time, which is similar to 3/4 time, or waltz time. Notice how we've used the open A string along with higher Am chord forms on the neck. This provides a nice, low-register bass note against which the higher voicings can move.

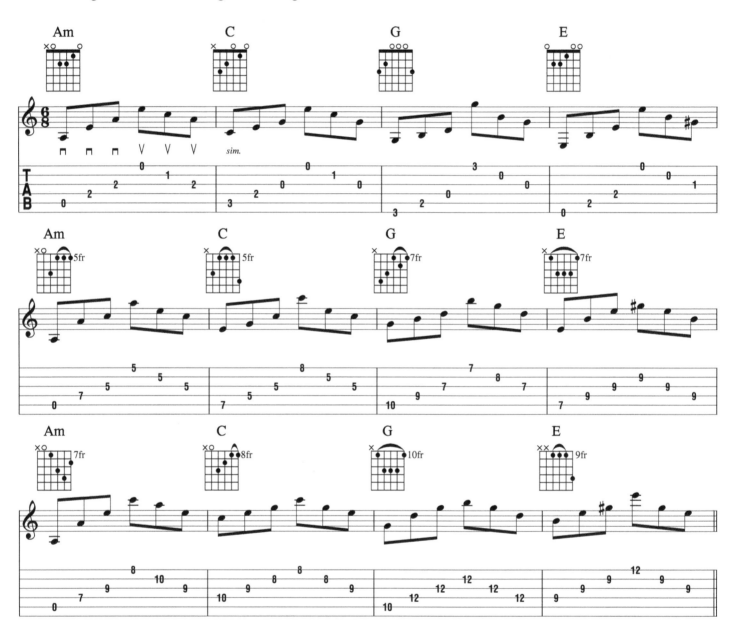

SONG 6

So far, we've been using the CAGED system to vary our chord shapes. However, we can also move the same shape around the fretboard. In **Song 6**, we use the same C-shape seventh chord to play C7, F7, and G7 chords. Note the alternating bass thrown in for additional interest.

SONG 7

TRACK 14

In **Song 7**, we're mixing triads with seventh chords. The A (I) and D (IV) chords are played as triads, while the V chord, E, is played as an E7.

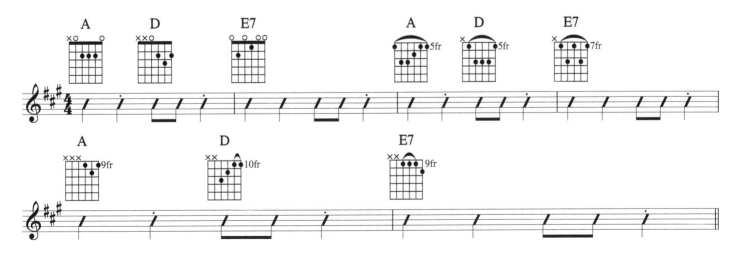

SONG 8

Here we're using hammer-ons to create chordal riffs on a Dm–Am–Gm progression.

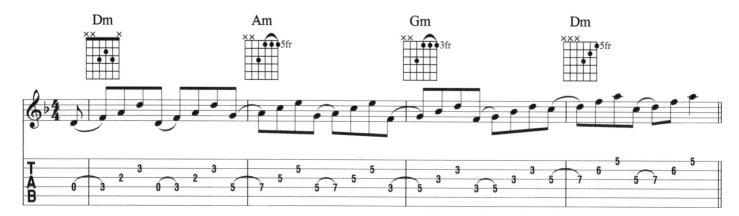

SONG 9

One of the many benefits of employing the CAGED system is the ability to compose multiple guitar parts. **Song 9** combines a driving, power-chord riff with an arpeggiated line for a full, interesting sound. A palm mute is applied to the power chords to further separate the two parts.

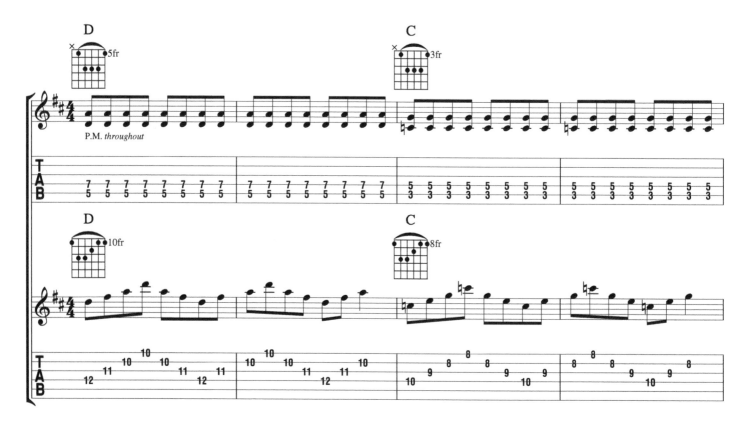

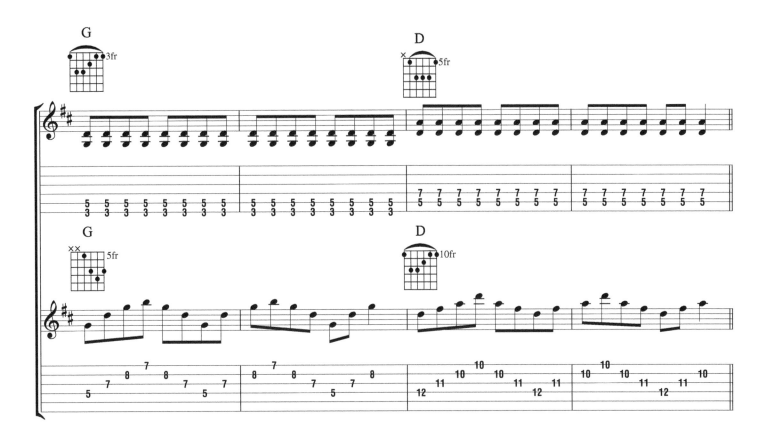

TRACK 17

SONG 10

In the same vein, check out this 12-bar blues in E. Guitar 1 plays a walking bass line riff that's fairly busy, so Guitar 2 complements it with some horn-like stabs while using different voicings. The blues can be pretty simple at times, but that doesn't mean it has to be boring.

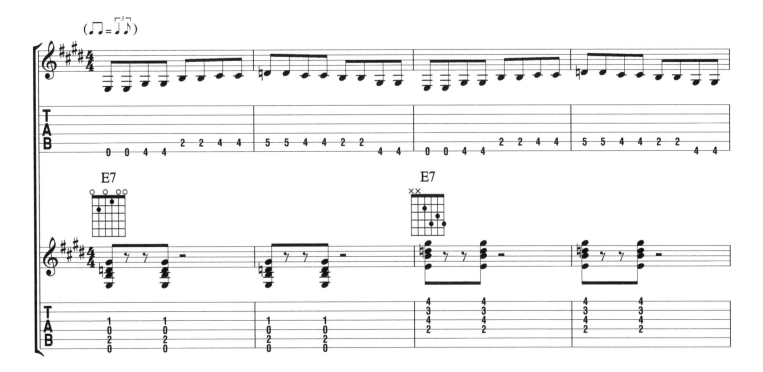

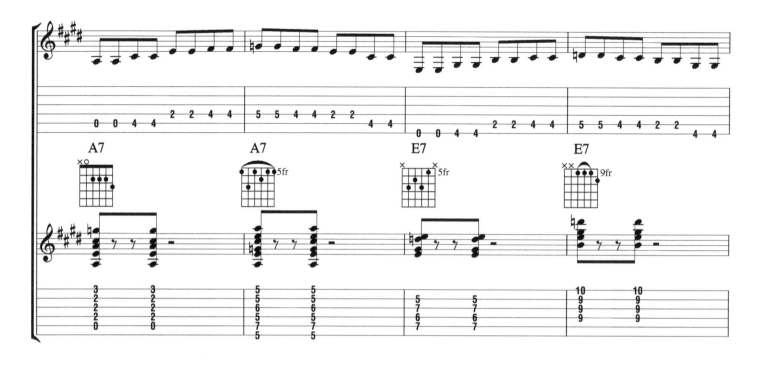

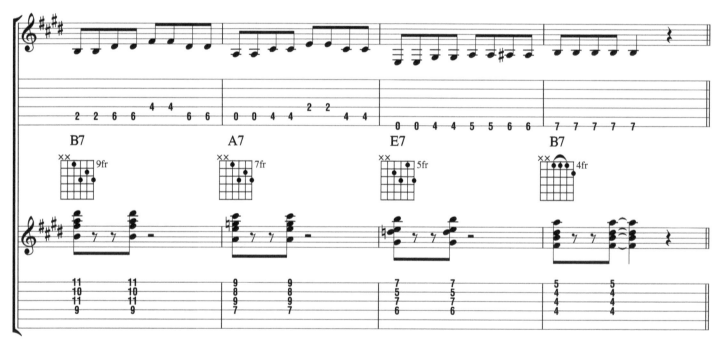

 **IRONWEED RAG**

TRACK 18

Here's one for the fingerpickers out there. If you don't fingerpick, you could pass this one up, but give a listen to the track, because it might inspire you to learn. I have found the CAGED system very useful in fingerpicking blues and ragtime tunes. It gives the player a lot of options to keep the music flowing in an interesting way without ever being boring.

This is a longer piece, but it has a fair amount of repetition. It's in the key of E and utilizes an alternating bass pattern that is primarily played between the 6th and 4th strings using the thumb of the right hand. It's basically a blues tune with an interesting turnaround that starts on C#7, the VI chord. I imagine that this will be the first stumbling block, as the chords run quickly to G, F#11, and B7. Work slowly through this passage; there is another version of it later on.

There are three passes through the verses, and each time the E chord becomes higher pitched, thus, hopefully sustaining interest. Notice how, in the second verse, moving the E chord up to a C shape opens up opportunities to play a nice slide and pull-off lick. In measure 22, we shift back to use a D-shape E7 that can be squished to make an E diminished chord. This was a popular move used by many early blues players, including Robert Johnson. The A7 passage in measure 26 incorporates a couple of extra notes: B and B♭. Don't let that mess with your head—those notes are really just extensions of the original A7.

When we reach the turnaround in measure 32, we play it twice. The first time is exactly like before, but the second pass takes the same chord progression and works it up the neck; 7th chords, 9th chords, and other extended chords like 13ths in this case are interchangeable, and the B13 chord operates like a B7.

In the third pass, we crawl even higher up the neck to a G-shape E7 that anchors itself at the ninth fret, and grab notes on the first string between the frets 12 and 9. One thing I like about all the different E and A chords we play in this song is that we can use a low open string (6 for E, 5 for A) combined with a higher bass note that keeps moving as we substitute different shapes. In measures 49–50, we once again use that diminished 7th chord change—this time for A7.

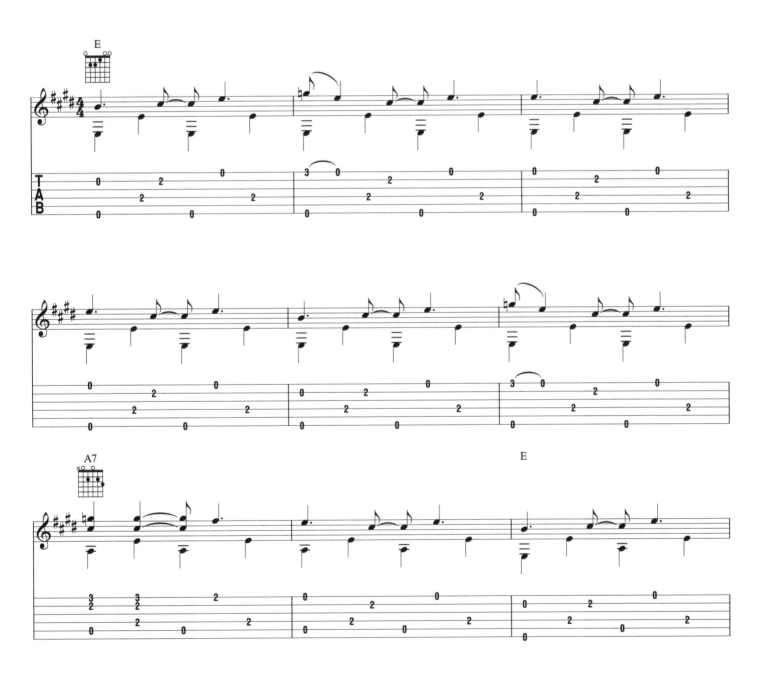

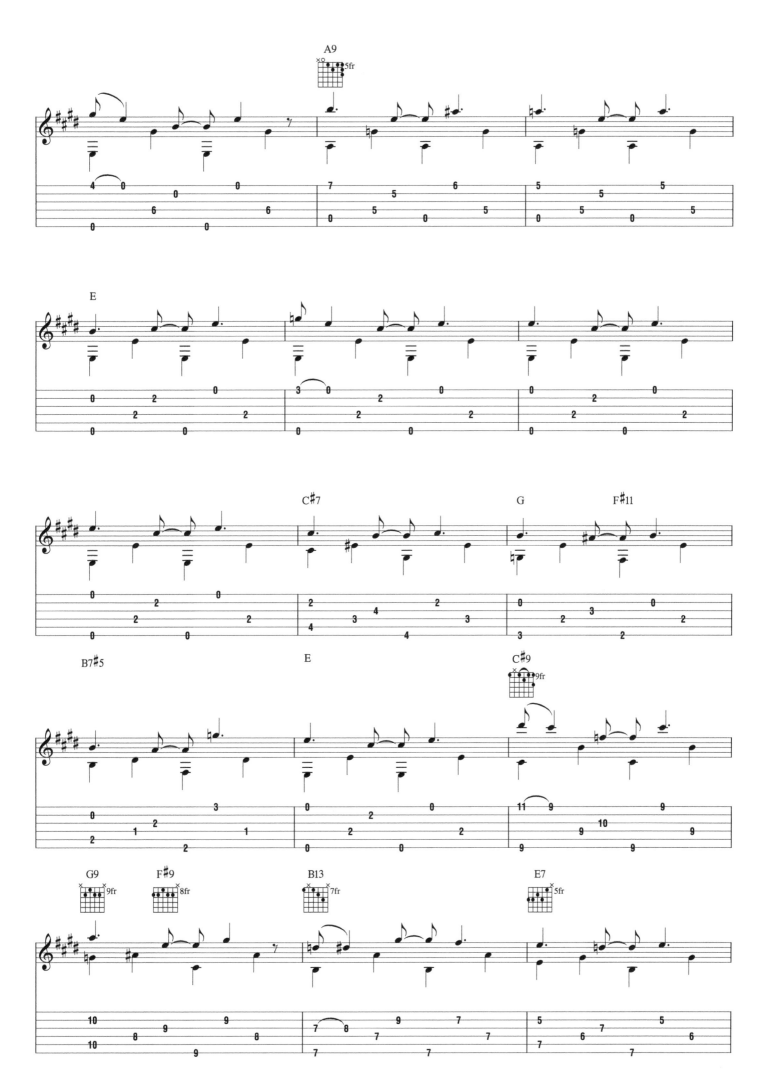

CHAPTER 5:
Shortcuts

As we saw earlier with the G shape, it is sometimes better to not play the full version of the chord. You may have already played some of these partial chords, not realizing that they are simply smaller versions of the chords in the CAGED system. There are many ways to make shortcuts for ourselves.

Here we've taken the "closed" position of each shape ("closed" meaning we are not playing any open strings) and one-by-one stripped away the lowest sounding string. Remember, we need just three notes to define a major or minor triad. So I can break each shape down to just three notes, or three strings being played. We will learn practical applications for this later on in the chapter.

You will notice that when we strip away the two lowest notes of the C shape it looks like the top three notes of a D shape; you could say that the D shape is actually imbedded in the C shape.

Major Triad Shortcuts

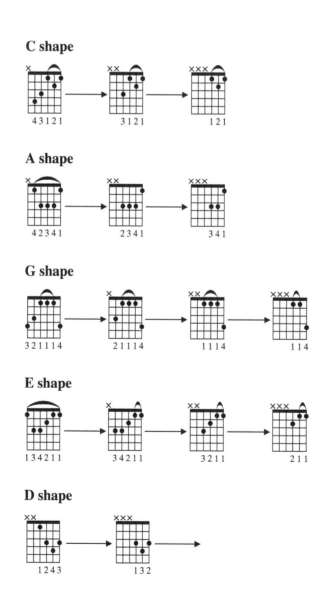

Minor Triad Shortcuts

C minor shape

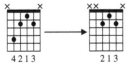

A minor shape

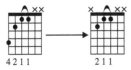

G minor shape

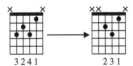

E minor shape

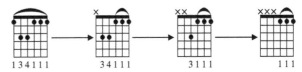

D minor shape

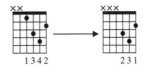

Seventh Chord Shortcuts

C7 shape

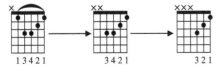

A7 shape

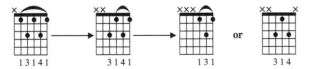

or

G7 shape

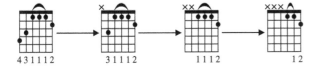

E7 shape

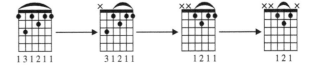

D7 shape

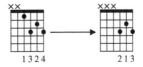

Shortcut Examples

The following exercises demonstrate how to use these smaller chord forms over progressions to create different rhythmic effects.

In **Example 1**, we've taken a typical C–F–G7 chord change using open chords for the first two measures. Then, we shift the first finger to barre at the fifth fret. This yields an A-shape C chord (try not to play the first string, or you will end up with a C6 chord), a C-shape F chord, and a D-shape G7 chord.

EXAMPLE 1

TRACK 19

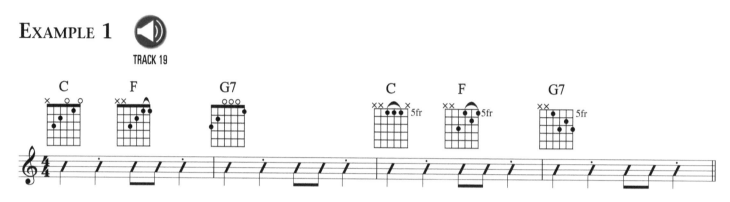

Here's an example of how small chords can make a big statement. We're playing in the upper register with a percussive, staccato attack. This type of part would sound great when combined with a lower-register keyboard or guitar part.

EXAMPLE 2

TRACK 20

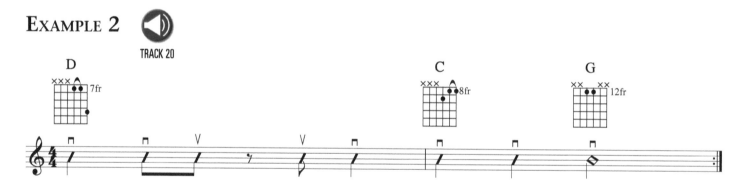

Example 3 is a funky rhythm part that uses small versions of an A-shape C chord and a C-shape F chord. These voicings are very similar to what was used in **Example 1**.

EXAMPLE 3

TRACK 21

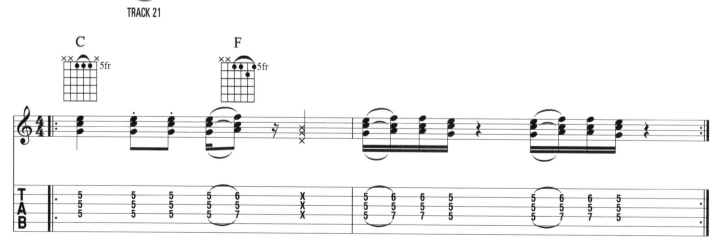

Example 4 is another funky little part that uses two small-form chords. In this case, we're in E, and using E7 (G shape) and A7 (D shape) chords.

EXAMPLE 4

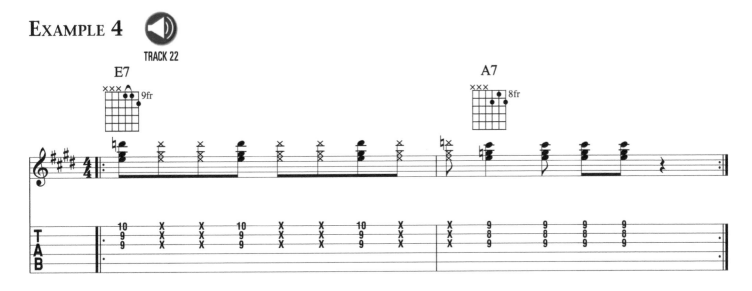

Example 5 uses a doo-wop progression and some shortened E-shape chords in the first two measures, combined with some shortened A-shape chords in the third and fourth measure to produce a light, feathery-type rhythm.

EXAMPLE 5

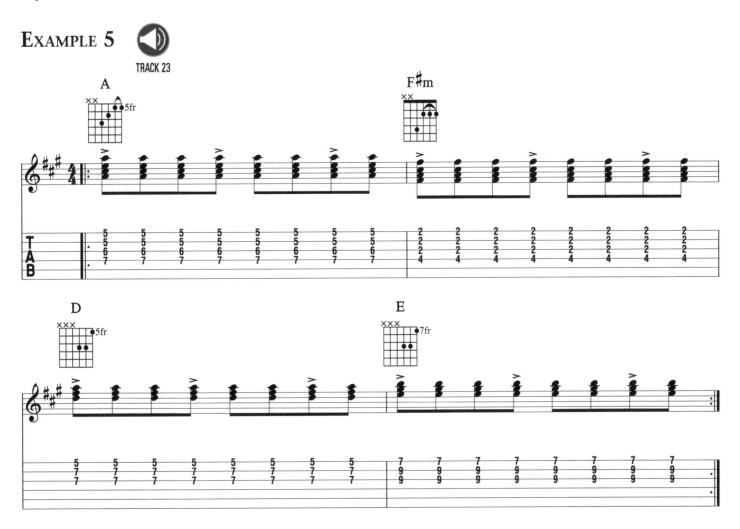

Example 6 has a Prince-like feel to it. We're combining E-shape G and F chords with a G-shape C7 chord.

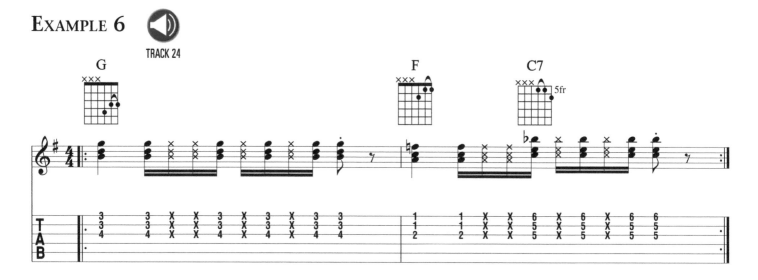

Example 7 is in 6/8 and has a bit of a power ballad feel to it. We begin with some high-register chords using A shapes (Em) and E shapes (Bm and A) and then make a sudden shift in register down to some power chords for the second half. Power chords don't contain a 3rd, which means they're technically neutral—neither major nor minor. However, we can imply the tonality of them because of the context we've been given earlier. We finish off with an arpeggio and a chromatic bass lick.

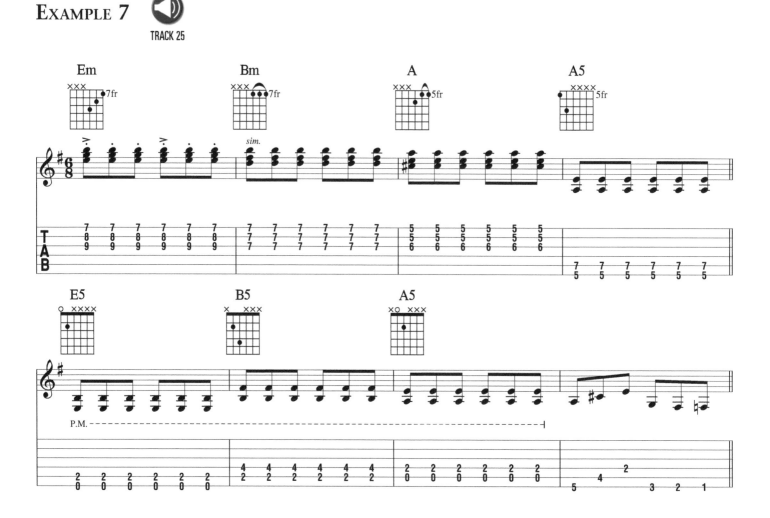

In **Example 8**, we're taking full E-shape versions of Am, F, and G chords and breaking them up into two-string forms (dyads) for each measure. The first two measures play out as power chords, although they're inverted in measures 3 and 4, with the 5th on the bottom and a root on top. In measures 3 and 4, the 3rds come into play.

EXAMPLE 8

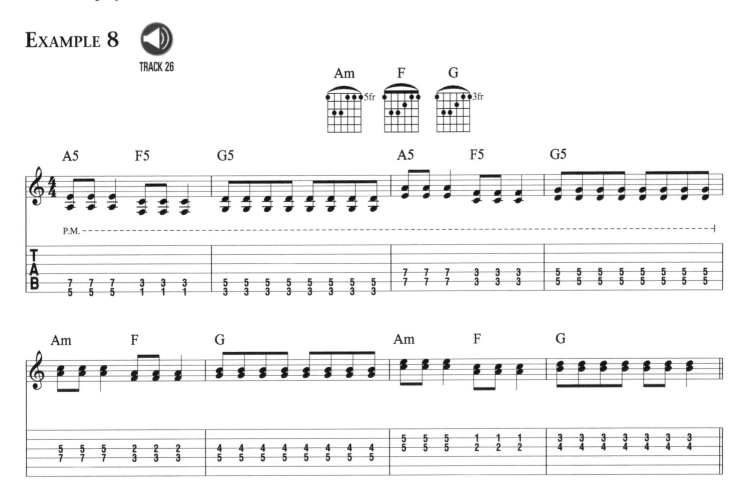

Example 9 uses mostly partial G and C shapes to create a surfy vibe. The E7 and D7 chords toward the end use the A shape.

EXAMPLE 9

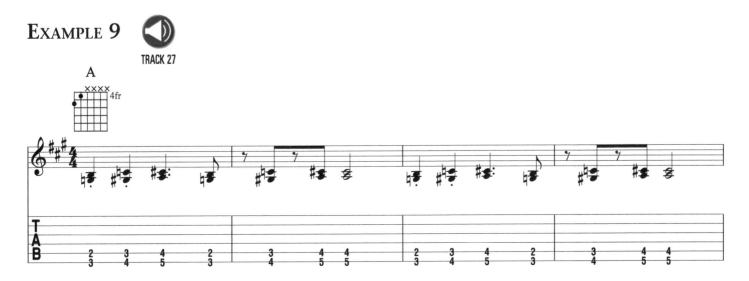

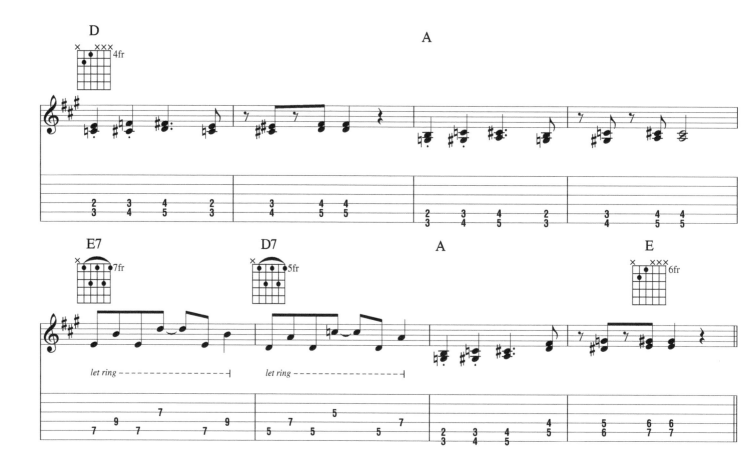

In **Example 10**, we're using small-form E and C shapes with a ringing open-E string to create some nice sounding chords: G6, D9, and C7. Be sure to allow the notes to ring together as much as possible for the proper effect.

EXAMPLE 10

TRACK 28

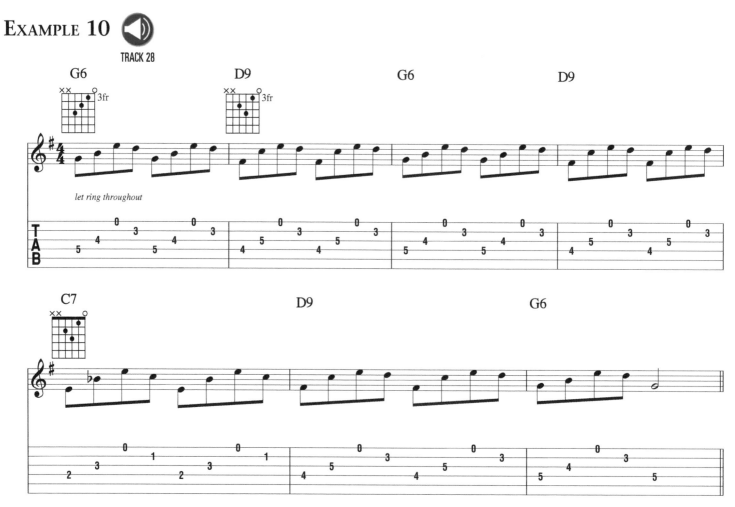

CHAPTER 6:
Riffs

Riffs are usually short, repeatable musical phrases that can be rhythmic or melodic in nature and have the quality of "hooking" the listener. Many of the examples from the previous chapter could qualify under that definition. You can think of this chapter as a continuation of that previous chapter, with the caveat that we have opened up the chords for larger, more expansive voicings. The chord shapes you use will often define the nature of your riffs. Small chords using just two or three strings can produce a powerful riff, while larger chords using more strings often lend themselves to more expansive and atmospheric riffs. Try these riffs out and, as always, expand on them and use the ideas to spur your own imagination.

RIFF 1

TRACK 29

This riff travels between an E-shape and a G-shape G chord via double stops. The slides help to impart a bluesy vibe and lend a Keith Richards feel to the riff. There are a few scale tones that aren't technically part of the chord, but I think you can see how they're related to the chord shapes without going into too much theory.

RIFF 2

TRACK 30

This bluesy riff takes an arpeggio fragment up through several different forms of E7: D shape, C shape, G shape, and E shape.

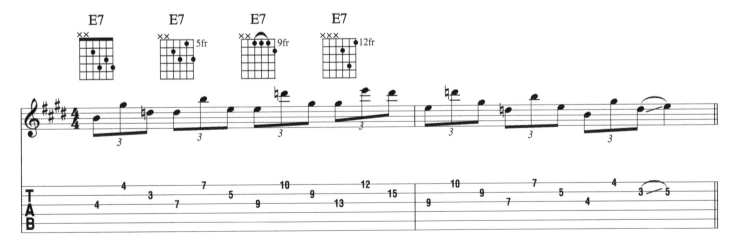

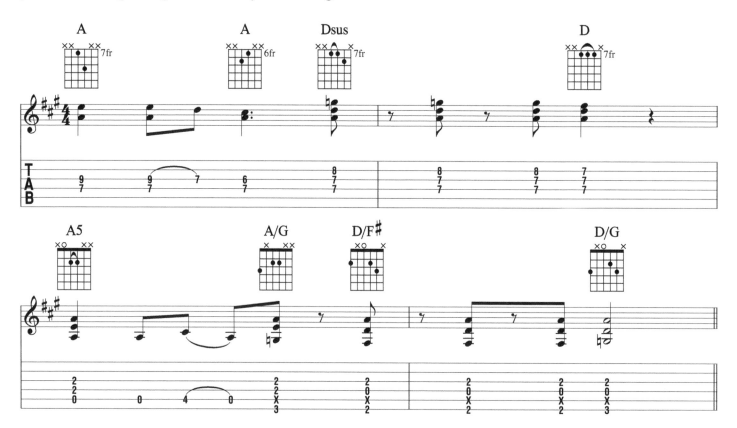

RIFF 3

TRACK 31

Our third riff has a power-rock feel to it and makes use of several inversions, suspensions, and slash chords (a chord over a different bass note) to create some very interesting sonorities. For example, in measure 3, we add a G bass note to an A power chord. This demonstrates how you can try out different notes based around your chord shapes to get some really interesting results.

RIFF 4

TRACK 32

This riff blends partial notes from a C shape and an A shape. We take the same chordal riff and move it up through a C–D–F–G progression.

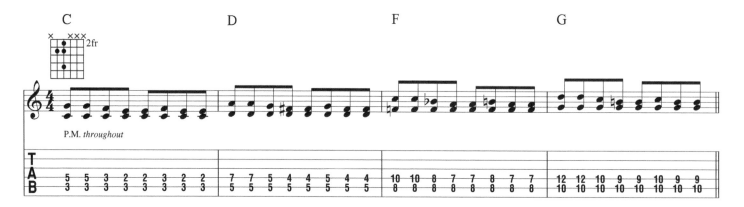

RIFF 5

In this John Lee Hooker-style riff, we're working around the open Am form, adding melody notes and bass line melodies to create a question-and-answer effect.

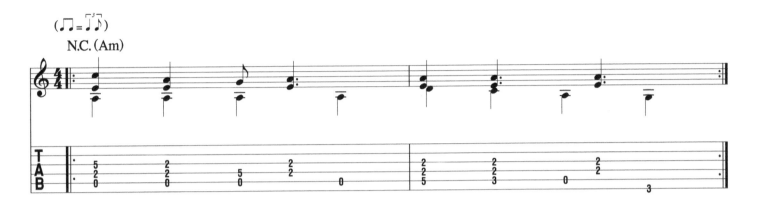

RIFF 6

This bluesy riff moves between an E-shape B7 chord and several forms of an E7 chord. Keep the bass notes muted to increase the separation between parts.

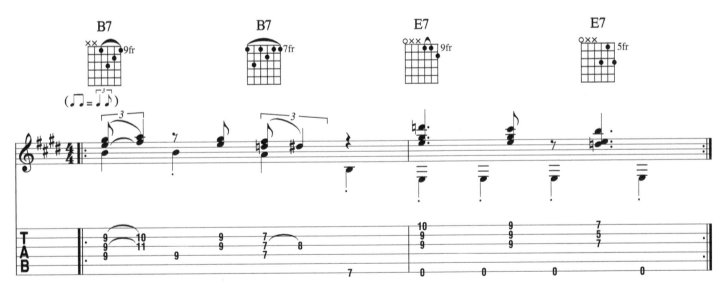

RIFF 7

In this country-style riff, we move between a G-shape and an E-shape B chord, adding some bluesy hammer-ons and slides along the way. In measures 1 and 3, fret the low B with your pinky; this sets you up nicely for the rest of the measure.

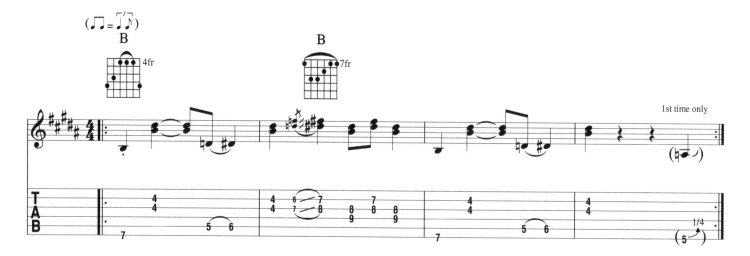

RIFF 8

This one has just a bit of a Beatles flavor to it. We're using some single-note additions to an A-shape D7 chord and an F-shape A chord, with the open G string employed to make it an A7.

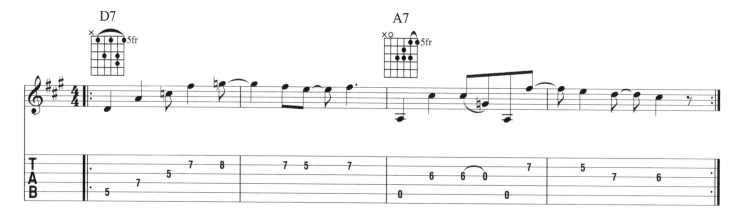

RIFF 9

This final example is as much of a song section as it is a riff. Again, in measures 1 and 2, we're using notes that aren't part of the chord but are closely related to the shape. You don't have to get too much into theory to play around with notes near the chord shapes and see what you come up with. After some pretty-sounding embellishments through a G–Em chord sequence, we finish off with some grittier power chords. Notice the passing B5 chord used to connect C5 and A5.

APPENDIX:
How to Study Theory

Theory, by itself, can be a very abstract subject. I recommend studying theory in conjunction with analyzing songs and solos of your favorite musicians. There are two aspects to studying theory: 1) the physical aspect, which involves getting your fingers to learn patterns and the memorization of those patterns; and 2) the intellectual aspect of understanding how the notes work together to make music. The intellectual understanding usually comes after the physical memorization, so in the beginning you will be spending most of your time simply memorizing scales and patterns—and probably cursing your guitar teacher for subjecting you to this! But if you persevere, you begin to see how all this stuff fits together, and the instrument (and your love for it) will seem to take on a life of its own.

I recommend that as you learn scales, you also incorporate riffs based on those scales. You should also record yourself playing different rhythms and soloing over them. This will be very humbling at first, but it is an invaluable tool to improving as a player.

In other words, studying theory should not be an independent venture, but should come in conjunction with your study of the instrument as a whole.

Theory and the CAGED System

The CAGED system is a visual system of shapes that can guide the player around the fretboard. However, eventually the player will probably ask, "How are these chords made?" Understanding how chords are built from a major scale is a tool you can take anywhere and to any instrument. Once you understand the relationships between the notes that make up these chords, your knowledge will transcend the guitar, and your understanding of music will increase your ability to communicate with musicians on any instrument. If you play in a band, you will find it very helpful to be able to convey your musical ideas in words and knowledge that musicians use every day.

The Major Scale

Most western music is based on the seven-note scale—Do Re Mi Fa Sol La Ti (Do)—as you may remember from elementary school (or *The Sound of Music*). While there are plenty of exceptions to this scale in modern western music, it is an invaluable place to start a discussion of music theory.

Let's begin by looking at the key of E, since guitar players, especially blues and rock players, play a lot in the key of E. There is another good reason for starting in E: the guitar's lowest and highest strings are both E, and this helps to see how scales and chords can be laid out in a linear fashion—progressing up the neck on either E string, we can clearly see how scale tones and chords are related to each other.

The scale tones of an E major scale are: E–F#–G#–A–B–C#–D#. To start with, let's play these notes on the low E string. Start with the open E, then play F# on fret 2, G# on fret 4, A on fret 5, B on fret 7, C# on fret 9, and D# on fret 11. Notice there is a pattern here. The space between the first scale tone (E) and the second scale tone (F#) is two frets; between the second (F#) and third (G#) notes is also two frets. Between the third and fourth tones (G# to A) is *one* fret; between the 4th and 5th (A to B) is two frets; from the 5th to 6th is two frets (B to C#); 6th to 7th (C# to D#) is two frets. Finally, to come back to the first scale tone, the octave E, we move one fret from D# to E.

As we said, the move from E to F♯ is two frets, but it is also two notes away: E–F–F♯. In music theory, this is called a *whole step*; any time we talk about moving up or down a whole step on one string, we are talking about a move of two frets. The move from the 3rd scale tone to the 4th scale tone (G♯ to A) is one fret, and that's called a *half step*. Any time we move one fret to the next fret above or below on one string, we are moving a half step. We'll abbreviate whole step as W and half step as H. The musical term for this—i.e., the distance between notes—is *interval*.

We can see that there is an intervallic formula for building a major scale. Looking at the E major scale:

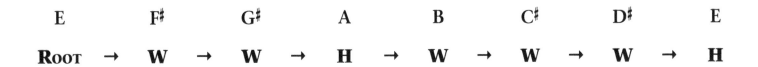

E is called the *root* because it is the root note of the key we are playing in: the key of E. But let's forget for a minute that we are playing in the key of E. We can transfer the above formula to any key:

Root	→	W	→	W	→	H	→	W	→	W	→	W	→	H
Root fret		2 frets		2 frets		1 fret		2 frets		2 frets		2 frets		1 fret
1		2		3		4		5		6		7		8

Notice that I have numbered each scale tone 1–7, with 8 being the octave. Let's play these scale tones in the key of F. Starting once again on the low E string, we can find F at the first fret. Using the same formula, we end up with this:

What you want to achieve here is a way to look at your fretboard and understand the relationship between notes.

Here is the intervallic formula for creating a major scale:

Major and Minor Chords

1	2	3	4	5	6	7	8
W	W	H	W	W	W	H	

The primary distinction between chords is whether they are major or minor. There are, of course, other distinctions, but by examining the major/minor relationships between the chords in a song, for example, we can determine which key we are in and know which scales and notes will fit that song.

The basis for building a chord is the major scale with which we've been working. We'll start by choosing three notes from the scale: the root, the 3rd, and the 5th. We call this group of notes a *triad* ("tri" meaning three). The distance from the root to the 3rd is four frets, or two whole steps. Another name for that distance is a major 3rd. We call it a 3rd because three note names are involved: the root, the 2nd, and the 3rd.

Root	2nd	Major 3rd
W	W	

It's called a major 3rd because it's part of a major chord, and the distance is four half steps.

When building a major chord, we skip over the second note of the scale; it is not needed. (We can use that second note later on to color or decorate our chord if we like.) Now we move from the 3rd to the 5th, which is a distance of three half steps, or one-and-a-half steps (a whole step plus a half step). This also called a *minor* 3rd: a distance of three half steps is a minor 3rd—the distance of three frets on one string as opposed to four frets for a major 3rd.

3rd	4th	5th
H	W	

The distance from the root (or first note) to the 5th is three-and-a-half steps: this is called a perfect 5th. It's called a 5th because five notes are involved in the interval: root, 2nd, 3rd, 4th, 5th.

If we look at the E major scale, E–F♯–G♯–A–B–C♯–D♯, we can pick out the 1st (root), 3rd, and 5th notes and that will be the basis for our E major triad. So, an E major triad is comprised of E, G♯, and B. Voila!

A minor chord, or minor triad, is very similar to a major triad. Instead of a major 3rd and a perfect 5th, we have a *minor* 3rd and a perfect 5th:

For example, E minor would have the notes E, G, and B, instead of E, G♯, and B. Another way of looking at it is that from E major to E minor, all you have to do is lower the third one half step (i.e., make the G♯ note a G♮).

Seventh Chords

Seventh chords—more specifically, dominant seventh chords—consist of four notes instead of three. They are formed by adding the ♭7th to a major triad. In forming our E major chord, we used the 1st, 3rd, and 5th notes of the E major scale (E–G#–B). The 7th note of the scale is D#. If we add D# to our chord, it becomes an E *major* 7th chord. This is another type of common seventh chord, but it's not a dominant seventh. To make E7 (E dominant 7th), we lower the 7th one half step to D♮. Dominant sevenths tend to sound somewhat unresolved, and they usually function as the V chord in a key. For example, in the key of E, you may see an E triad as the I chord, an A triad as the IV chord, and maybe a B7 as the V chord. It is an extremely useful chord for blues, rock, and jazz.

Chord Relationships Within the Major Scale

We've already numbered the scale tones 1–7, but you might also see a numbering scheme that uses Roman numerals.

E	F#	G#	A	B	C#	D#
1	2	3	4	5	6	7
I	ii	iii	IV	V	vi	vii°

The lower row of numerals represents the quality of chord that relates to the scale tone in that key. When I say "quality," I'm referring to either major or minor. Look at the bottom row a little more closely and you might notice that some of the numbers are uppercase, and some are in lowercase—there is a reason for this. The uppercase numbers refer to major chords and the lowercase numbers refer to minor. For instance, playing in the key of E major, we already know that E is a major chord, but we can also see that, using our theory model, the chord related to the 4th scale tone (A) is also major, and so is the 5th (B). The 2nd (F#), 3rd (G#), and 6th (C#) chords will all be minor. And the 7th chord (D#) is actually *diminished*, which is the same thing as a minor triad with a flat 5th. The symbol for diminished is °.

So, the *diatonic* (which just means "in the key") triads of E major are:

E	F#m	G#m	A	B	C#	D#°
I	ii	iii	IV	V	vi	vii°

This means that if you come across a song that's in E major, you're very likely to see several of these chords. There are plenty of exceptions, and you'll see chords other than these—the explanation for which is beyond the scope of this appendix. However, this is a good starting point from which to build.

Remember, this formula works for any major key. All you have to do is build the major scale for the key you want using the W W H W W W H formula, and you'll know the diatonic chords for that key by using the above Roman numeral formula.

For example, we can build a D major scale from the open D string. Following our formula, we end up with these notes for the D major scale:

D	E	F#	G	A	B	C#	D
	W	W	H	W	W	W	H

And by plugging in our Roman numeral formula, we can determine that the diatonic chords in this key are:

D	Em	F#m	G	A	Bm	C#°
I	ii	iii	IV	V	vi	vii°

The music theory world stretches far beyond this, but you're now equipped with a foundation on which to build in years to come.

AFTERWORD

The CAGED system can be a powerful tool for navigating the fretboard. Try experimenting with it—break up the chord shapes into smaller pieces. I think you will find that this gives your guitar playing an added punch. Have fun and get creative!

Get Better at Guitar

...with these Great Guitar Instruction Books from Hal Leonard!

101 GUITAR TIPS
STUFF ALL THE PROS KNOW AND USE
by Adam St. James
This book contains invaluable guidance on everything from scales and music theory to truss rod adjustments, proper recording studio set-ups, and much more.

00695737 Book/Online Audio $17.99

AMAZING PHRASING
by Tom Kolb
This book/audio pack explores all the main components necessary for crafting well-balanced rhythmic and melodic phrases. It also explains how these phrases are put together to form cohesive solos. The companion audio contains 89 demo tracks, most with full-band backing.

00695583 Book/Online Audio $22.99

ARPEGGIOS FOR THE MODERN GUITARIST
by Tom Kolb
Using this no-nonsense book with online audio, guitarists will learn to apply and execute all types of arpeggio forms using a variety of techniques, including alternate picking, sweep picking, tapping, string skipping, and legato.

00695862 Book/Online Audio $22.99

BLUES YOU CAN USE
by John Ganapes
This comprehensive source for learning blues guitar is designed to develop both your lead and rhythm playing. Includes: 21 complete solos • blues chords, progressions and riffs • turnarounds • movable scales and soloing techniques • string bending • utilizing the entire fingerboard • and more.

00142420 Book/Online Media.................................$22.99

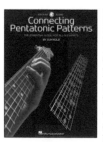

CONNECTING PENTATONIC PATTERNS
by Tom Kolb
If you've been finding yourself trapped in the pentatonic box, this book is for you! This hands-on book with online audio offers examples for guitar players of all levels, from beginner to advanced. Study this book faithfully, and soon you'll be soloing all over the neck with the greatest of ease.

00696445 Book/Online Audio $24.99

FRETBOARD MASTERY
by Troy Stetina
Untangle the mysterious regions of the guitar fretboard and unlock your potential. This book familiarizes you with all the shapes you need to know by applying them in real musical examples, thereby reinforcing and reaffirming your newfound knowledge.

00695331 Book/Online Audio $22.99

GUITAR AEROBICS
by Troy Nelson
Here is a daily dose of guitar "vitamins" to keep your chops fine tuned! Musical styles include rock, blues, jazz, metal, country, and funk. Techniques taught include alternate picking, arpeggios, sweep picking, string skipping, legato, string bending, and rhythm guitar.

00695946 Book/Online Audio $24.99

GUITAR CLUES
OPERATION PENTATONIC
by Greg Koch
Whether you're new to improvising or have been doing it for a while, this book/audio pack will provide loads of delicious licks and tricks that you can use right away, from volume swells and chicken pickin' to intervallic and chordal ideas.

00695827 Book/Online Audio $19.99

PAT METHENY – GUITAR ETUDES
Over the years, in many master classes and workshops around the world, Pat has demonstrated the kind of daily workout he puts himself through. This book includes a collection of 14 guitar etudes he created to help you limber up, improve picking technique and build finger independence.

00696587...$17.99

PICTURE CHORD ENCYCLOPEDIA
This comprehensive guitar chord resource for all playing styles and levels features five voicings of 44 chord qualities for all twelve keys – 2,640 chords in all! For each, there is a clearly illustrated chord frame, as well as *an actual photo* of the chord being played!.

00695224...$22.99

RHYTHM GUITAR 365
by Troy Nelson
This book provides 365 exercises – one for every day of the year! – to keep your rhythm chops fine tuned. Topics covered include: chord theory; the fundamentals of rhythm; fingerpicking; strum patterns; diatonic and non-diatonic progressions; triads; major and minor keys; and more.

00103627 Book/Online Audio $27.99

SCALE CHORD RELATIONSHIPS
by Michael Mueller & Jeff Schroedl
This book/audio pack explains how to: recognize keys • analyze chord progressions • use the modes • play over nondiatonic harmony • use harmonic and melodic minor scales • use symmetrical scales • incorporate exotic scales • and much more!

00695563 Book/Online Audio $17.99

SPEED MECHANICS FOR LEAD GUITAR
by Troy Stetina
Take your playing to the stratosphere with this advanced lead book which will help you develop speed and precision in today's explosive playing styles. Learn the fastest ways to achieve speed and control, secrets to make your practice time really count, and how to open your ears and make your musical ideas more solid and tangible.

00699323 Book/Online Audio $22.99

TOTAL ROCK GUITAR
by Troy Stetina
This comprehensive source for learning rock guitar is designed to develop both lead and rhythm playing. It covers: getting a tone that rocks • open chords, power chords and barre chords • riffs, scales and licks • string bending, strumming, and harmonics • and more.

00695246 Book/Online Audio $22.99

Guitar World Presents
STEVE VAI'S GUITAR WORKOUT
In this book, Steve Vai reveals his path to virtuoso enlightenment with two challenging guitar workouts – one 10-hour and one 30-hour – which include scale and chord exercises, ear training, sight-reading, music theory, and much more.

00119643...$16.99

HAL•LEONARD®